D0537344

LET'S EXPLORE THE STATES

Lower Plains

Kansas
Nebraska

Elisabeth Herschbach

Mason Crest
450 Parkway Drive, Suite D
Broomall, PA 19008
www.masoncrest.com

©2016 by Mason Crest, an imprint of National Highlights, Inc.

Printed and bound in the United States of America.

CPSIA Compliance Information: Batch #LES2015.
For further information, contact Mason Crest at 1-866-MCP-Book.

First printing
1 3 5 7 9 8 6 4 2

Library of Congress Cataloging-in-Publication Data

Herschbach, Elisabeth.
  Lower plains : Kansas, Nebraska / Elisabeth Herschbach.
    pages cm. — (Let's explore the states)
  Includes bibliographical references and index.
  ISBN 978-1-4222-3326-9 (hc)
  ISBN 978-1-4222-8611-1 (ebook)
  1. Middle West—Juvenile literature. 2. Kansas—Juvenile literature.
  3. Nebraska—Juvenile literature. I. Title.
  F351.H57 2015
  978—dc23
                                2015000178

Let's Explore the States series ISBN: 978-1-4222-3319-1

Publisher's Note: Websites listed in this book were active at the time of publication. The publisher is not responsible for websites that have changed their address or discontinued operation since the date of publication. The publisher reviews and updates the websites each time the book is reprinted.

About the Author: Elisabeth Herschbach, an editor, writer, and translator, lives in Maryland with her Kansas-born husband, Michael, and their son, Alexander.

Picture Credits: courtesy Gerald R. Ford Library: 56 (bottom); Independence National Historical Park, Philadelphia: 18 (bottom); Library of Congress: 16, 18 (bottom), 19, 20, 23, 28 (top, center), 48, 56 (top); Mighty Sequoia Studio: 17; Minerva Studio: 12; Nagel Photography: 25 (top, bottom right); National Archives: 21 (bottom), 22, 43, 45, 46; National Park Service: 41; Allen Graham/PDImages: 15; used under license from Shutterstock, Inc.: 6, 7, 14, 27 (top), 34, 35, 60, 61; Gary L. Brewer/Shutterstock.com: 30; Tommy Brison/Shutterstock.com: 32; George Burba/Shutterstock.com: 1, 5 (bottom); Ann Cantelow/Shutterstock.com: 38 (top); Sharon Day/Shutterstock.com: 39, 41; Philip Eckerberg/Shutterstock.com: 51; Bart Everett/Shutterstock.com: 13 (bottom); Featureflash/Shutterstock.com: 28 (bottom); David Lee/Shutterstock.com: 9; Marekuliasz/Shutterstock.com: 54; Daniel J. Rao/Shutterstock.com: 5 (top); J. Norman Reid/Shutterstock.com: 27 (bottom); Henryk Sadura/Shutterstock.com: 52; Weldon Schloneger/Shutterstock.com: 38 (bottom), 49, 55; Sue Smith/Shutterstock.com: 31; R. Thoma/Shutterstock.com: 58; John Ray Upchurch/Shutterstock.com: 21 (top); Max Voran/Shutterstock.com: 11; Michael Vorobiev/Shutterstock.com: 10; U.S. Department of Defense: 29, 53, 57; U.S. Department of Health and Human Services: 26; U.S. Fish and Wildlife Services: 13 (top); Visions of America: 25 (bottom left), 37, 40, 47, 50, 59.

Table of Contents

KEY ICONS TO LOOK FOR:

Words to Understand: These words with their easy-to-understand definitions will increase the reader's understanding of the text, while building vocabulary skills.

Sidebars: This boxed material within the main text allows readers to build knowledge, gain insights, explore possibilities, and broaden their perspectives by weaving together additional information to provide realistic and holistic perspectives.

Research Projects: Readers are pointed toward areas of further inquiry connected to each chapter. Suggestions are provided for projects that encourage deeper research and analysis.

Text-Dependent Questions: These questions send the reader back to the text for more careful attention to the evidence presented there.

Series Glossary of Key Terms: This back-of-the book glossary contains terminology used throughout this series. Words found here increase the reader's ability to read and comprehend higher-level books and articles in this field.

LET'S EXPLORE THE STATES

Atlantic: North Carolina, Virginia, West Virginia
Central Mississippi River Basin: Arkansas, Iowa, Missouri
East South-Central States: Kentucky, Tennessee
Eastern Great Lakes: Indiana, Michigan, Ohio
Gulf States: Alabama, Louisiana, Mississippi
Lower Atlantic: Florida, Georgia, South Carolina
Lower Plains: Kansas, Nebraska
Mid-Atlantic: Delaware, District of Columbia, Maryland
Non-Continental: Alaska, Hawaii
Northern New England: Maine, New Hampshire, Vermont
Northeast: New Jersey, New York, Pennsylvania
Northwest: Idaho, Oregon, Washington
Rocky Mountain: Colorado, Utah, Wyoming
Southern New England: Connecticut, Massachusetts, Rhode Island
Southwest: New Mexico, Oklahoma, Texas
U.S. Territories and Possessions
Upper Plains: Montana, North Dakota, South Dakota
The West: Arizona, California, Nevada
Western Great Lakes: Illinois, Minnesota, Wisconsin

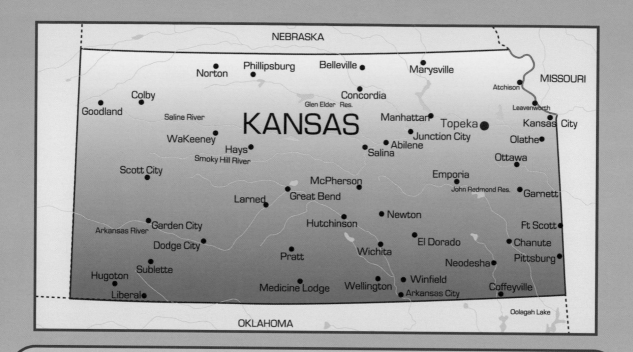

 Kansas at a Glance

Area: 82,278 sq miles (213,099 sq km)[1]
  15th-largest state.
  Land: 81,759 sq mi (211,755 sq km)
  Water: 519 sq mi (1,344 sq km)
Highest elevation: Mount Sunflower,
  4,041 feet (1,232 m)
Lowest elevation: Verdigris River at
  Oklahoma border, 679 feet (207 m)

Statehood: Jan. 29, 1861 (34th state)
Capital: Topeka

Population: 2,904,021
  (34th largest state)[2]

State nickname: The Sunflower State
State bird: Western meadowlark
State flower: Wild sunflower

[1] *U.S. Census Bureau*
[2] *U.S. Census Bureau, 2014 estimate*

Kansas

D rive through the Kansas countryside in late summer and you'll see fields of golden blooms lining the roadside. These are the flowers that gave the Sunflower State its official state nickname. But Kansas also has a slew of other nicknames that capture different aspects of its history and character. Kansas is sometimes called the Midway State, because it contains the geographical center of the 48 *contiguous* American states. It is called the Wheat State because it is one of the country's major producers of this vital grain. And it is called the Jayhawker State after the abolitionists who fought to keep slavery out of Kansas during the 19th century.

Geography

Measuring just over 82,000 square miles (213,099 square kilometers), Kansas is the 15th-largest state in the nation and the third largest in the Midwest. Shaped like a rectangle with a bite taken out of the top-right corner, Kansas is bounded by four states: Colorado on the west, Missouri on the east,

Nebraska on the north, and Oklahoma on the south.

The Kansas landscape is commonly thought of as flat and *monotonous*. Contrary to the stereotype, however, Kansas as a whole isn't really flat. There are deep valleys and steep slopes in some parts of the state. The elevation can change as much as 400 feet (122 m) in a single area. Kansas's lowest point is at the Verdigris River in the southeast. The elevation here is 679 feet (207 m). The state's highest elevation is 4,041 feet (1,232 m) at Mount Sunflower, along the western border with Colorado.

The High Plains region, stretching across the western third of the state, is the area that most closely fits the stereotypical image of Kansas. A vast

Words to Understand in This Chapter

confluence—the place where two rivers or streams join up.

conquistador—a soldier in the Spanish conquests of the Americas in the 16th century.

contiguous—adjacent, or sharing a common border.

guerrilla warfare—irregular warfare carried out by small, independent groups of fighters.

monotonous—lacking variety; boring and unchanging.

popular sovereignty—the right of settlers in a territory to decide by vote whether or not to permit slavery.

reservoir—an artificial lake used for storing water.

sediment—sand, soil, and rock particles deposited by water, wind, or glaciers.

temperance movement—a movement beginning in the early 19th century advocating the restriction or prohibition of alcoholic beverages.

thwart—to prevent someone from doing something; to defeat their plans.

topography—the features of a land area, such as mountains and rivers.

A farm's windpump on the Kansas prairie. Since the 19th century, windpumps have been used on the Great Plains to pump water from farm wells for cattle.

expanse of open, windswept prairieland, this is Kansas's driest and flattest region. The High Plains were once carpeted with a lush lawn of short green grass. Millions of buffalo (bison) grazed here in great herds. When white settlers moved in, much of the prairie was plowed up and the buffalo were killed off. Today, cattle graze in their place.

The Smoky Hills region in north-central Kansas is home to the Monument Rocks, also called the Chalk Pyramids. These are a group of striking chalk formations, sometimes as tall as 70 feet (21 m) high. They were created some 80 million years ago during the Cretaceous Period, when most of Kansas was covered by a shallow inland sea. Scientists have discovered extensive fossil deposits in the chalk beds, including the remains of extinct species of fish, flying reptiles, and prehistoric birds.

Most of eastern Kansas lies in the fertile Central Lowlands. Some 600,000 years ago, glaciers covered this part of the state. Massive sheets of ice, some as thick as 500 feet (152 m), moved across the landscape from the north. In the process, rocks and soil were transported hundreds of

The chalk (soft limestone) deposits that form Monument Rocks were created 80 million years ago, when this region was part of a vast inland sea. Today abundant fossilized remains of shells and ancient sea creatures can be found here.

miles from their origin. When the glaciers melted, this *sediment* was deposited, creating the rich soils that make this area so good for farming.

The Flint Hills area in the east-central part of the state is characterized by sloping hills and rolling grasslands. It is prime pastureland for cattle. The area gets its name from the flint deposits in the limestone underlying the hills. These deposits made the soil too rocky to be plowed up and converted to farmland, as was done in Illinois and other prairie states. As a result, Flint Hills has the nation's largest remaining tallgrass prairie preserve. At one time, the United States had some 142 million acres (57.5 million hectares) of tallgrass prairie. Now less than 5 percent of that remains, most of it here in Flint Hills.

Just as Kansas's **topography** varies across the state, so too does the climate. Eastern Kansas has hot, humid summers and cold winters. In the west, summers are less humid and winters are subject to wild fluctuations and extremes.

Northeastern Kansas averages about 35 inches (89 cm) of rain per year and enjoys the longest growing season in the state. Western Kansas, by contrast, receives only 16 to 20 inches (41 to 51 cm) of rainfall a year. The wettest part of the state is the Ozark Plateau in the southeast, where up to 46 inches (117 cm) of rain can fall per year. Average snowfall in Kansas ranges from less than 5 inches (13 cm) in the south of the state to up to 35 inches (89 cm) in the northwest.

Kansas is prone to severe thunder-

The Flint Hills in southeast Kansas were named because large amounts of flint can be found throughout the region. The prairie in this area still looks as it did before the arrival of Europeans.

Kansas is known for its tornadoes, which occur when rapidly swirling winds in a thunderstorm form a funnel cloud that can cause great damage wherever it touches down. The winds of a tornado can exceed 300 mph (483 kph). According to the National Weather Service, the annual number of tornadoes in Kansas has been increasing since the late 1980s. The most tornadoes occurred in 2008, when more than 180 of these powerful storms ravaged the Sunflower State.

storms, blizzards, and windstorms—not to mention the tornadoes made famous by *The Wizard of Oz*. This is because of its location on open plains where cold air from the north of the continent meets warm air from the south. The state is also vulnerable to periodic droughts and flooding.

To control flooding, many lakes and reservoirs were built in the 1950s. Almost all of Kansas's major lakes, in fact, are manmade. The largest is Milford Lake, a 16,000-acre (6,475 ha) reservoir constructed by damming the Republican River to control flooding from the Republican and Kansas rivers.

One of Kansas's few naturally formed lakes is Cheyenne Bottoms in central Kansas. But although the lake basin itself is natural, manmade dams and canals have been added to control the water levels. These were constructed to provide wetlands for migratory birds. About 45 percent of all migrating shorebirds in North America pass through these marshy waters. As many as 328 different species of birds have been observed here. That number includes several endangered species, such as the pere-

A flock of Marbled Godwit shorebirds gather together at the Quivira National Wildlife Refuge located in Stafford.

The Arkansas River meanders over the plains north of Wichita.

Mount Sunflower, located near the western border with Colorado, is the highest point in Kansas. Because the state's terrain gradually rises from east to west, the "summit" is virtually indistinguishable from the surrounding area. It is 4,039 feet (1,231 m) above sea level.

grine falcon, whooping crane, and bald eagle. Cheyenne Bottoms is the largest inland wetland in the United States.

Kansas is also home to one of the longest prairie rivers in the nation: the Kansas River in the northeast of the state. Also known as the Kaw, the Kansas River served as an important transportation hub for pioneers moving into the frontier. Other important rivers include the Missouri River, which forms 75 miles (121 km) of Kansas's northeastern border with Missouri State, and the Arkansas River, which snakes across western and southern Kansas for nearly 500 miles (800 km).

History

Kansas is named after the Kansa, or Kaw, tribe of Indians. They migrated west from the Ohio Valley in the early 1700s, ending up in what is now northeastern Kansas. The Kaw, or "People of the South Wind," lived in villages along the river valleys, where they cultivated corn, beans, and squash. Periodically, they left their villages to hunt buffalo in the western reaches of the state.

By the mid-18th century, the Kaw had become the dominant tribe in Kansas. Before their arrival, however, the area was occupied by Pawnee and Wichita Indians. These were the tribes that the first European explorers encountered when they arrived here in 1541, led by the Spanish *conquistador* Francisco Vasquez de Coronado.

Coronado's interest in the Plains

The Keeper of the Plains is a 44 foot (13 m) tall steel sculpture, located in Wichita near the spot where the Arkansas and Little Arkansas rivers meet. The sculpture, by a Kiowa-Comanche artist named Blackbear Bosin, was completed in 1974. Nearby are exhibits about the various Native American tribes that inhabited this region before the arrival of Europeans in the 16th century.

was piqued by tales of a mythical city of gold called the "Kingdom of Quivira." Coronado and his men trudged for more than a month across prairieland, from Texas to Oklahoma to Kansas. Eventually they found Quivira. It turned out to be a few villages of Wichita Indians living in grass huts in central Kansas—no gold in sight. With their hopes for treasure dashed, the Spanish packed up and went home.

The next serious attempts to explore Kansas came almost two centuries later. This time it was French explorers who came seeking to establish trade relations with the Indians along the Missouri River. The French traded European goods, including guns, metal tools, and alcohol. In exchange, they wanted fur.

Across Europe, North American furs—especially beaver furs—were in big demand. As a result, many French trappers made great fortunes from the fur trade. The Indians did not fare so well. Contact with Europeans exposed them to new diseases. Epidemics of smallpox and other infectious diseases devastated their numbers.

By the end of the 1600s, France had acquired a vast stretch of land

Statue of the Spanish explorer Francisco Coronado in the city of Liberal, in southwestern Kansas. In the 1540s, Coronado led a small Spanish army through the Great Plains in search of seven legendary cities of gold.

west of the Mississippi River. This area, called Louisiana after King Louis XIV, included present-day Kansas. Territorial disputes with Great Britain, however, led to the outbreak of the French and Indian War in 1754. In order to ***thwart*** Great Britain, France ceded all of this territory, including Kansas, to its ally Spain in 1762.

France regained the area from Spain in 1800. Three years later, however, the United States bought it from the French as part of the Louisiana Purchase. President Thomas Jefferson soon ordered an expedition into the newly acquired lands. Captain Meriwether Lewis and Lieutenant William Clark were put in charge. Between 1804 and 1806, they covered more than 8,000 miles (12,875 km). Their goal was to explore and map the territory, chart a route westward to the Pacific Ocean, and develop trade relations with local Indian tribes.

Lewis and Clark first reached Kansas in June of 1804—just over a month into their expedition. They camped at the ***confluence*** of the Kansas and Missouri rivers, along

Lewis and Clark spent a short time in Kansas during their 1804–06 exploration of the Louisiana Purchase. In their notes, they wrote about the abundance of game and the beauty of the prairie.The spot where their group originally camped for several days, Kaw Point, is near present-day Kansas City.

what today is Kansas's northeastern border. On July 4, they celebrated Independence Day in present-day

Atchison. They gave nearby Independence Creek its name in honor of the occasion.

In 1806, a young army lieutenant named Zebulon Pike led a second expedition through Kansas. Pike journeyed through southeastern, central, and western Kansas. He then followed the Arkansas River west into Colorado. In his reports, he described Kansas as dry, barren, and unsuitable for settlement.

Zebulon Pike

In large part because of Pike's unfavorable reports, there was very little white settlement in the area until the 1850s. Instead, the area was designated as "Indian Country."

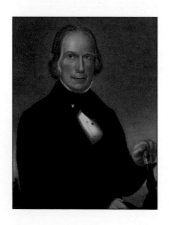

Henry Clay (1777–1852) was an influential political leader in the early 19th century. He represented Kentucky in Congress, and ran for president several times. Clay helped to formulate the Missouri Compromise in 1820.

As part of the Indian Removal Act of 1830, more than 25 Indian tribes were moved into the Kansas region. This was done to make way for increased white settlement in the East. These tribes included the Shawnee, Delaware, Potawatomi, Wyandot, Kickapoo, and Ottawa, among others. Later, when settlement of Kansas began in earnest, many of these tribes were again forced to move, this time to Oklahoma.

By the late 1840s, interest in Kansas began to pick up. Two of the major transportation routes of the 19th century traveled through Kansas: the Santa Fe Trail and the Oregon-California Trail. Thousands of wagons rumbled through, carrying settlers and goods westward. Some of these settlers decided to stay in Kansas, instead of traveling farther. As their numbers increased, there was a push to organize Kansas into a U.S. territory.

In 1854, Congress passed the Kansas-Nebraska Act. This created the two new territories of Kansas and Nebraska. The bill also repealed the Missouri Compromise of 1820, which

This political cartoon from 1856 blames the Democratic Party for violence in Kansas in the years after the 1854 Kansas-Nebraska Act. It depicts a bearded "free-soiler" (someone who opposed slavery in the Kansas Territory) being held down by Democratic Party politicians James Buchanan and Lewis Cass, while two other Democrats, Senator Stephen A. Douglas and President Franklin Pierce, force a black man (representing slavery) down his throat.

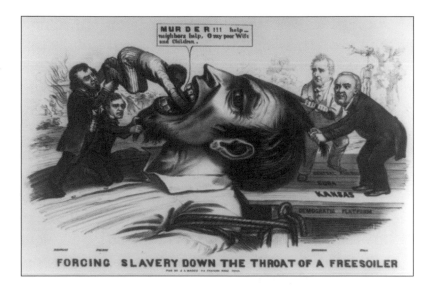

had banned slavery in the lands of the Louisiana Purchase north of the 36° 30´ latitude line. Under the Kansas-Nebraska Act, the two territories would instead be allowed to decide their position on slavery by *popular sovereignty*.

Kansas quickly became a battleground between pro-slavery and anti-slavery factions. Abolitionist settlers poured into the new territory, hoping to secure its future as a free state. Pro-slavery Missourians—known as "border ruffians"—crossed into Kansas to harass the settlers and vote illegally.

All too often, violent clashes broke out. The violence became so bad that the term "Bleeding Kansas" was coined to describe the new territory.

The worst bloodshed came in 1856. The town of Lawrence, an anti-slavery stronghold, was raided by a mob of border ruffians. In

John Brown

retaliation, abolitionist John Brown led an attack on a pro-slavery camp near Pottawatomie Creek, killing five men.

Ultimately, the abolitionists were

successful. Kansas entered the Union as a free state on January 29, 1861, becoming the 34th state. Less than three months later, however, the Civil War broke out. The slavery issue, which had split "Bleeding Kansas" into warring factions, was now tearing apart the nation as a whole.

Most of the fighting in Kansas was **guerrilla warfare**. Deadly raids across the Kansas-Missouri border continued to occur. Once again, the town of Lawrence was a target. On August 21, 1863, confederate guerrillas led by William Clark Quantrill burned the town down and killed almost 200 people.

The most significant military battle to occur in Kansas was the Battle of Mine Creek. Fought in October 1864, this was one of the largest cavalry battles of the war. It was a decisive loss for the Confederates and one of the last major battles fought west of the Mississippi River.

The decades after the Civil War were boom years for Kansas. In 1860, Kansas's population was just over 100,000. By 1880, the population had reached one million. Most of the set-

This drawing, published in a magazine in 1863, shows the attack on Lawrence by Quantrill's Confederate raiders during the Civil War. Quantrill planned the attack in retaliation for Union attacks on pro-slavery towns in neighboring Missouri. More than 180 civilians—most of Lawrence's adult male population—were massacred during the raid, and much of the town was burned.

tlers came from other U.S. states and territories. Many also came from Europe, especially Germany and the British Isles.

Starting in the 1870s, large numbers of black settlers migrated to Kansas, escaping the South in search of a better life. These settlers became known as Exodusters, after the exodus from Egypt in the Bible.

Fueling Kansas's boom was the expansion of the railroads. Construction of the first railroad line to pass through the state, the Kansas Pacific Railroad, began in 1863. The Kansas Pacific later became part of the Union Pacific Railroad, which crossed the entire country. By the end of the 19th century, Kansas was ranked third in the nation for rail mileage, with almost 9,000 miles (14,500 km) of railroads crisscrossing the state.

Thanks to the railroads, a thriving cattle industry developed in Kansas. From the mid-1860s to the mid-1880s, hundreds of thousands of cattle were herded every year from Texas to Kansas. These cattle were then

A restored Union Pacific Railroad engine on display in Dodge City.

A 19th-century cowboy rounds up cattle on a ranch near present-day Kansas City.

This photo of "peace commissioners" in Dodge City, circa 1883, includes some of the West's most iconic lawmen and gunfighters. Pictured are (front, left to right) Charlie Bassett, Wyatt Earp, Frank McLain, Neal Brown, (back) W.H. Harris, Luke Short, and Bat Masterson.

 ## Did You Know?

In 1887, Susanna Salter became the first American woman elected to political office when she won the race for mayor in the southern Kansas town of Argonia. That very year, Kansas had just granted women the right to vote and run for office in city elections.

shipped by rail to the east. Dodge City in southwestern Kansas became one of the largest cattle markets in the world. Major cattle hubs also sprang up in Abilene, Wichita, Newton, and Ellsworth. These cowtowns developed a reputation for lawlessness and violence, with rowdy saloons and drunken cowboys slinging guns.

Not surprisingly, these saloons drew the fire of the growing ***temperance movement*** in Kansas. One of the most famous members of this movement was Carrie A. Nation. She raided taverns and saloons across the state, attacking them with a hatchet. In 1881, Kansas became the first state in the nation to ban alcohol. Prohibition against alcohol lasted until 1948 in Kansas, longer than in any other state.

Even after the cowtown era came to a close, cattle continued to play an important role in Kansas's economy. Livestock production and meatpacking became major industries in the state. But 19th-century Kansas's biggest business was farming. As waves of pioneers settled across the state, vast expanses of prairie were plowed up to plant crops. Kansas quickly established itself as one of the nation's top farm states. By the mid-1880s, flour milling had become its leading industry.

Kansas' agricultural boom was a mixed blessing. In good years, many farmers prospered. But cultivating the prairie left the land vulnerable to a serious problem: dust storms. The prairie grass had acted as a natural protective barrier against erosion. Without the thick roots of the grass to hold the soil in place, the plowed land was exposed to the strong winds of the Plains. When periods of drought hit, the fragile topsoil blew away in great clouds of dust.

The 1930s were a period of severe

A huge cloud of dust can be seen behind the buildings in the city of Elkhart, in southwestern Kansas, May 1937. A series of droughts during the 1930s were compounded by the use of farming methods that were not appropriate for the Great Plains. These created the conditions for massive dust storms, and ultimately resulted in thousands of Kansas families having to abandon their unprofitable farms.

drought and dust storms. Historians refer to this period as the Dust Bowl. All of the Plains states were affected, from Texas to the Dakotas. But southwestern Kansas was hit especially hard. Dust clouds up to two miles high swept across the Plains. Some topsoil was blown as far away as New York City. Many farmers went bankrupt.

In the 1950s, a century after the "Bleeding Kansas" era, the Jayhawker State once again became a battle zone for civil rights. This time, however, the battle was in the courts. Although slavery had long been abolished in the nation, many states still practiced racial segregation. These states, including Kansas, maintained a policy of "separate but equal." Under this policy, it was legal to require blacks to use separate facilities from whites, as long as these facilities provided the same services.

Oliver Brown, an African-American father from Topeka, Kansas, challenged this policy of racial segregation when he tried to enroll his daughter in an all-white school. When she was denied the chance to enroll, Brown took the case to court. Ultimately, the landmark case *Brown v. Board of Education* went to the U.S. Supreme Court. In 1954, the Court ruled that the policy of "separate but equal" was unconstitutional, ending the practice of school segregation nationwide.

Government

Kansas has a bicameral, or two-chamber, state legislature consisting of the Kansas Senate and the State House of Representatives. Its 40 state senators are elected to four-year terms and its 125 state representatives serve two-year terms.

Kansas's executive branch consists of six elected officials who each serve

 Did You Know?

The nation's first patented helicopter was built in 1909 in Goodland, Kansas. William J. Purvis and Charles A. Wilson, two railroad mechanics, got the idea for their design from watching a child playing with a pinwheel.

(Right) The state legislature meets in this building in Topeka. The building was constructed in 1903. In early 2014 a $325 million project to renovate the capitol building was completed.

(Bottom right) The Kansas House of Representatives meets in this chamber inside the capitol building.

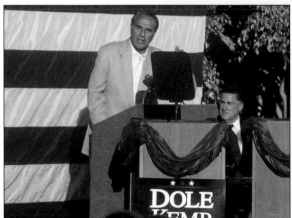

Robert "Bob" Dole represented Kansas in the U.S. House of Representatives from 1961 to 1969, and in the U.S. Senate from 1969 to 1996. He is pictured here giving a speech during his 1996 presidential campaign.

Kathleen Sebelius was the second woman elected governor of Kansas, serving in that post from 2003 to 2009. She then took a cabinet position under President Barack Obama as Secretary of Health and Human Services from 2009 until 2014.

four-year terms: the governor, lieutenant governor, secretary of state, attorney general, state treasurer, and insurance commissioner. The governor appoints the Kansas Supreme Court's seven justices.

In addition to its two U.S. senators, Kansas sends four U.S. representatives to Congress. Republicans have dominated both local and national politics throughout its history. As of 2014, Kansas has not elected a Democrat to the U.S. Senate for over 80 years.

In the early 2000s, Kansas's State Board of Education made headlines twice for controversial rulings on evolution. First, the Board voted to eliminate evolution from state curriculum standards. Later, it voted to require science teachers to spend an equal amount of time teaching both the theory of evolution as well as "intelligent design," a pseudo-scientific theory that an intelligent being (God) created all things and guided evolution. Although both of these decisions were reversed, they reinforced Kansas's reputation for being more politically conservative than much of the nation.

The Economy

Historically, farming has been Kansas's biggest industry. Currently, however, other industries play a larger role in the state's overall economy. According to the U.S. Department of Commerce, Kansas's gross domestic product (GDP) was $144.1 billion in 2013. The finance, government, and service industries accounted for the biggest share of that.

Kansas also has a robust manufacturing industry. More than half of the nation's general aviation airplanes are manufactured here. Cessna, a major producer of business jets, is headquartered in Wichita.

Nonetheless, Kansas is still a major farm state. The U.S. Department of Agriculture counted more than 61,000 farms in Kansas in 2012. In fact, farms make up about 90 percent of the state's total land area. Kansas ranks number one in the nation for wheat production and flour milling. It is also the nation's top producer of sorghum, one of the world's oldest crops. It is thought that sorghum was first brought to the United States on a slave ship from Africa in the late 1700s. Today, the U.S. uses the grain primarily for animal feed. Other major crops grown in Kansas include corn, soybeans, sunflowers, and alfalfa hay.

Kansas's biggest source of agricultural revenue comes from cattle—a legacy of the state's 19th century cowtowns. It is the nation's third largest producer of cattle. Kansas also has a multi-million dollar meatpacking industry.

Central Kansas, in particular, is rich in mineral resources, including oil, coal, and natural gas. According to the Kansas Geological Survey, Kansas pumped about 3.8 million barrels of

An oil pump in a Kansas wheat field. The state has become one of America's leading producers of oil and natural gas.

A large grain elevator and fertilizer tanks near Alexander.

Some Famous Kansans

Born just outside of Manhattan in northeastern Kansas, William Chrysler (1875–1940) started his career as a mechanic in the railroad town of Ellis. He went on to found the Chrysler Corporation, the seventh largest auto manufacturer in the world, maker of Dodge, Jeep, and other popular cars.

Dwight D. Eisenhower

Dwight Eisenhower (1890–1969) may have been born in Texas, but the 34th president of the United States spent his childhood in Abilene in the Flint Hills region of Kansas.

Atchison-born Amelia Earhart (1897–1939) was the first woman to fly solo across the Atlantic Ocean. In 1937, her plane disappeared over the Pacific Ocean. The mystery of her disappearance still has not been solved.

Amelia Earhart in the cockpit of her Lockheed Electra airplane.

A key figure in the Harlem Renaissance, poet Langston Hughes (1902–1967) was born in Missouri but raised in Lawrence, Kansas. He was one of the first writers to experiment with jazz poetry, a style of poetry that replicates the rhythm and feel of jazz.

Kansas City-born jazz icon Charlie Parker (1920–1955) left a lasting musical legacy as the inventor of bebop.

Singer-songwriter Melissa Etheridge (b. 1961) released her twelfth album, *Fourth Street Feeling*, in 2012. The title references a street in her hometown of Leavenworth.

Best known for his appearances on *Saturday Night Live*, Overland Park native Jason Sudeikis (b. 1975) got his start as an actor and comedian by performing at ComedySportz in Kansas City.

Jason Sudeikis

crude oil in 2013. That puts the state at tenth place in the nation for oil production.

In 1887, oil-seekers discovered salt deposits in central Kansas. The state continues to be a major salt producer, and the Independent Salt Company in Kanopolis, Kansas, is America's oldest continuously operating salt mine.

The People

Travel books and sites often describe Kansas as a land of open spaces. That is fitting. Although Kansas is the 15th largest state in terms of land area, it ranks only 34rd in terms of population. The 2010 U.S. Census put Kansas's population at 2,853,116. That comes out to an average of 34.9 people per square mile. By contrast, the average for the nation as a whole is 87.4 people per square mile.

Compared to the nation as a whole, Kansas is also less ethnically and racially diverse. The Census found that 87.1 percent of Kansans are white. The national average is just under 78 percent. African Americans are 13.2 percent of the overall U.S. population, but only 6.2 percent of Kansas's population. Just over 17 percent of Americans are of Hispanic or Latino heritage. In Kansas, the percentage is only 11.2 percent.

Fort Leavenworth is the oldest U.S. Army fort in the western United States still in existence. Today, it is best known for housing the U.S. Army Command and General Staff College, where high-ranking officers are trained, as well as a military prison. There are two other major U.S. military installations in the state, McConnell Air Force Base and Fort Riley.

View of Wichita, Kansas, on the Arkansas River.

Kansas also has a smaller proportion of residents born in a foreign country—almost exactly half the national average. Mexico, Germany, and Vietnam are the most common countries of origin for foreign-born Kansans.

Major Cities

More than 380,000 people make their home in *Wichita*, Kansas's largest city. From being a major cowtown in the 19th century, Wichita turned into the "Air Capital of the World." The city gave itself that grandiose title in the 1920s and 1930s, when a large number of aircraft companies set up business here. During World War II, Wichita was a manufacturing base for Boeing B-29 bombers. Today, the city remains an important hub of the U.S. aircraft industry.

A whopping 2.34 million people live in the Kansas City metropolitan area. But most of those people are actually Missourians, not Kansans. The metropolitan area spans both states, stretching over a total of 15 counties. Kansas City, Missouri, forms the biggest chunk of the metropolitan area. Its population is close to 460,000. **Kansas City, Kansas**, is much smaller. Just over 145,000 people live here. Other notable cities in Kansas's share of the metropolitan area are **Overland Park** and **Olathe**. The Kansas City metropolitan area as a whole hosted a thriving jazz scene in the 1920s and 1930s. Nowadays, it is famous for its barbecue.

To the west of Kansas City is **Topeka**, the capital of the state. It's Kansas's fourth-largest city, with over 127,000 residents. Located along the Kansas River, Topeka boasts a number of important historical landmarks, including the *Brown v. Board of Education* National Historic Site.

The city of **Lawrence** was once a hotbed for jayhawkers—the abolitionists who clashed with slavery supporters across the Missouri-Kansas border in the "Bleeding Kansas" era. Today,

This marker near the town of Lebanon indicates the geographic center of the contiguous United States.

Lawrence (population about 88,000) is home to the Kansas University Jayhawks. That's the nickname for KU's sports teams and their fans. One of the most famous Jayhawks was Dr. James Naismith, the inventor of basketball. He was a faculty member at KU, Kansas's largest public university, from 1898 to 1937.

Kansas's sunflowers, which reach their maximum height during August, are not just pretty flowers. Their seeds are harvested and used as food, or to produce sunflower oil.

Further Reading

Nault, Jennifer. *Kansas: The Sunflower State*. New York: Weigl Publishers, 2012.

Reece, Richard. *Bleeding Kansas*. Minneapolis: ABDO Publishing Co., 2012.

Stallard, Mark. *Tales from the Kansas Jayhawks Locker Room: A Collection of the Greatest Jayhawks Basketball Stories Ever Told*. New York: Sports Publishing, 2012.

Internet Resources

http://www.kgs.ku.edu/Extension/home.html

Find out more about the geology of Kansas, including its fossils, on the information-packed GeoKansas website.

http://www.kshs.org

The Kansas Historical Society provides a wealth of educational materials on the state's history and heritage at its website.

http://www.kshs.org/portal_kansapedia

Browse this searchable online encyclopedia to find more information about specific topics in Kansas history.

http://www.ameliaearhartmuseum.org

The Amelia Earhart Museum's website includes information about the legendary pilot, as well as a digitized archive of historic newspaper clippings from the 1920s and 1930s.

 # Text-Dependent Questions

1. Why was the territory of Kansas referred to as "Bleeding Kansas" in the 19th century?
2. What factors contributed to the Dust Bowl?
3. Name three of Kansas's top agricultural products.

 # Research Project

Through the Indian Removal Act of 1830, the federal government moved more than 10,000 Native Americans from the East into lands west of the Mississippi. Using the Internet or your school library, learn more about the tribes that were moved into Kansas. Pick one or two of these tribes to research in more depth. Find out more about their history, cultural traditions, and original lands, as well as the challenges they faced after removal to Kansas.

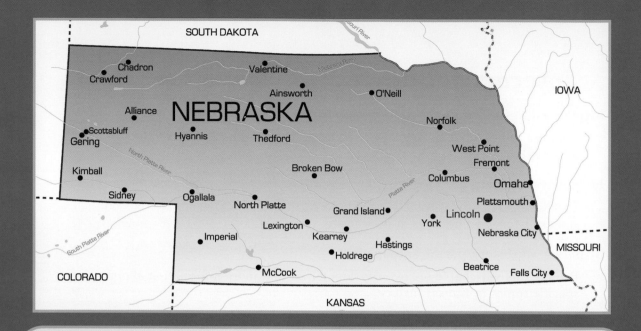

 ## Nebraska at a Glance

Area: 77,348 sq miles (200,330 sq km)[1]
   (16th largest state)
   Land: 76,824 sq mi (198,973 sq km)
   Water: 524 sq mi (1,357 sq km)
Highest elevation: Panorama Point,
   5,424 feet (1,653 m)
Lowest elevation: Missouri River at
   Kansas border, 840 feet (256 m)

Statehood: March 1, 1867
   (37th state)
Capital: Lincoln

Population: 1,881,503
   (37th largest state)[2]

State nickname: The Cornhusker State
State bird: Western meadowlark
State flower: Goldenrod

[1] *U.S. Census Bureau*
[2] *U.S. Census Bureau, 2014 estimate*

Nebraska

In 1820, Major Stephen H. Long led the first scientific exploration into Nebraska. He journeyed along the Platte River, exploring the area's natural resources and geography. At the end of his journey, he concluded that much of Nebraska was unfit for settlement and utterly unsuitable for agriculture. On the map, he labeled the area as a great desert.

That's not altogether surprising. Much of Nebraska is treeless. Large stretches have no running streams. But Nebraska is a good example of the motto that appearances can be deceiving. Thanks to rich soils and an underground *aquifer* with great stores of water, Nebraska actually has some of the nation's best farmland. Today, Nebraska is one of America's top corn producers, as reflected in its nickname—the Cornhusker State.

Geography

Nebraska covers 77,348 square miles (200,330 square kilometers) in the heartland of the United States. It is the nation's 16th largest state by area. South Dakota lies to the north, and Kansas is on the south. Colorado's border cuts into the southwestern corner of Nebraska at a right angle. This forms Nebraska's *panhandle*, a strip of land extending westward from the main portion of the state. Wyoming borders the panhandle on the west. The Missouri River makes up Nebraska's entire eastern border with Iowa and Missouri.

One of the Missouri River's most important *tributaries* is the Platte River, which crosses through the center of the state. French explorers Pierre and Paul Mallet gave the river its name in 1739, based on the French word meaning "flat." The Oto Indians, who lived in the area at the time,

Words to Understand in This Chapter

aquifer—an underground layer of rock or soil that stores extractable water.

badlands—a barren terrain where erosion has carved rock formations into striking shapes.

commodity—a product that is bought and sold.

encroachment—the gradual takeover of something that belongs to another person.

indigenous—native to a particular region or environment.

irrigation—the artificial application of water to the land to help in growing crops.

nomadic—moving from place to place without having a fixed home.

nonpartisan—not affiliated with any particular political party or group.

panhandle—a strip of land projecting out from the main territory of one state into that of another.

reservation—an area of public land set side for use by a Native American tribe.

semi-sedentary—living in a settled place for most of the year, but moving around and living in temporary homes for the rest of the year.

transcontinental—crossing an entire continent, from one end to the other.

tributary—a river or stream that flows into a larger one.

Two major waterways—the North Platte River and the South Platte River—meet in western Nebraska to form the Platte River, which then flows across the state to the Missouri River.

called it "Nebrathka," meaning "shallow water."

True to its name in both languages, the Platte River is relatively shallow and broad. As a result, it made an easy crossing point for 19th-century pioneers heading westward in covered wagons.

The shallow channels of the river also make ideal roosting grounds for sandhill cranes. Every year, up to half a million of the birds—more than 80 percent of the world's sandhill crane population—rest here for a few weeks during their spring migration.

Other major rivers in Nebraska are the Niobrara River, flowing through the north of the state, and the

Sandhill cranes wade in the shallow Platte River. The Platte and its tributaries (North and South Platte) flow for more than 1,000 miles (1,600 km).

This easternmost region is also called the Dissected Till Plains. "Till" refers to the rich sediment left behind by the Ice Age glaciers that once covered this part of Nebraska. When the glaciers melted, erosion from the run-off water dissected, or cut, the land into rolling hills and crisscrossing streams. Much of eastern Nebraska is farm country, but the state's biggest cities, Omaha and Lincoln, are also located here.

The Great Plains region is sub-divided into a number of smaller sections with their own distinctive features.

Republican River, flowing through the south. In total, Nebraska has over 23,000 miles (37,000 km) of rivers, streams, and canals. Most of its rivers drain into the Missouri River.

Nebraska can be divided into two main land regions: the Great Plains and the Central Lowlands. Most of Western Nebraska lies in the Great Plains, the vast region of plains stretching between the Mississippi River and the Rocky Mountains. The Central Lowlands make up the eastern fifth of the state.

Hilly fields planted with corn near Schuyler. Eastern Nebraska is known for its fertile soil.

View of the Sandhills region of Nebraska, which covers about one-fourth of Nebraska. The sandy soil here is not suitable for growing crops, although the grasses that anchor the dunes in place can be used for grazing. As a result, the Sandhills are a productive region for cattle ranching.

The Rainwater Basin in south-central Nebraska contains thousands of clay-lined basins that trap rainwater to form shallow marshes and wetlands. These sink-like basins—created by wind erosion some 27,000 years ago—attract large numbers of birds stopping through on their northward migration. In early spring, millions of snow geese congregate here.

In the north-central part of Nebraska is the roughly 20,000-square-mile (51,800 sq km) Sandhills area. This is North America's largest area of sand dunes. In addition to the dunes, more than one thousand shallow lakes dot the landscape here.

The Sandhills area also has Nebraska's largest stores of groundwater, supplied by the Ogallala Aquifer. This vast *reservoir* of water stretches underground from South Dakota to Texas. Groundwater provides nearly two-thirds of the water used in Nebraska for *irrigation*. Irrigation allows farmers to grow crops on lands once considered too dry for agriculture.

Extending across Nebraska's panhandle is the High Plains region. In general, this area is flat and covered with a stubble of short prairie grasses. In places, sharp ridges and other rock formations jut up over the landscape. At the western edge of the High Plains are two low groups of pine-forested mountains: Pine Ridge and the Wild Cat Hills.

Chimney Rock, one of Nebraska's most famous landmarks, is in the High Plains region. Towering almost 300 feet (91 m) above ground, it was visi-

Chimney Rock rises above the North Platte River valley in western Nebraska. During the 19th century, it was a prominent landmark for settlers traveling west. Today the Nebraska State Historical Society manages the land around Chimney Rock, and operates a visitors center that has exhibits and information about the pioneers who passed through this region.

View of western Nebraska from Scott's Bluff.

ble for days to the pioneers traveling along the Oregon Trail in the mid-19th century.

Toadstool Park in the northwest is an area of **badlands**. Here, wind and water have carved the landscape into steep slopes and interesting shapes—some even resembling toadstools, as the name suggests. Many fossils have been discovered in this area, including fossils from a prehistoric species of pig.

In the far southwestern corner of the panhandle is Nebraska's highest natural point: Panorama Point. It has an elevation of 5,426 feet (1,654 m) above sea level. By contrast, the state's lowest point is in the far southeast of the state, where the Missouri River meets Nebraska's border with Kansas. There, the elevation is 840 feet (256 m) above sea level.

Nebraska's panhandle is the driest region of the state. It typically receives less than 14 inches (36 cm) of rainfall a year. The eastern part of the state gets almost twice that amount of rain. This explains why eastern Nebraska

Scotts Bluff was an important landmark on the westward pioneer trails of the 19th century. The region contains several bluffs (steep hills) on the south side of the North Platte River; Scotts Bluff is the largest, rising more than 800 feet (240 m) above the surrounding area.

has a bigger population and more farmland than western Nebraska. Across the state as a whole, however, precipitation can vary greatly from season to season and year to year.

Much like Kansas, Nebraska also experiences extremely variable temperatures. The occasional freak blizzard can hit in late spring, while January might turn unexpectedly balmy. Typically, however, summers are hot and winters are cold throughout the state. It is not uncommon for summer temperatures to top 100°F (38°C) across Nebraska. In the northwest, winter temperatures sometimes dip as low as –20°F (–29°C). Also like Kansas, Nebraska has a history of tornadoes, floods, droughts, and dust storms.

History

Gold is what brought the first European explorers into the Plains region in the 16th century, when tall tales of treasure lured Coronado into present-day Kansas. Gold is also what brought the first large numbers of European Americans into Nebraska some 300 years later—gold in California mines more than a thousand miles away.

A pioneer family is photographed with their wagon while traveling to their homestead in the Loup Valley of Nebraska, circa 1886.

When the precious metal was discovered in California in 1848, a rush of prospectors trekked across the country to seek their fortunes. Their route passed through Nebraska, following the Platte River into the foothills of the Rockies. This was part of the eastern leg of the 2,000 mile (3,200 km) Oregon-California Trail. Wagons ferried tens of thousands of people across Nebraska. Supplies and freight moved up and down the Platte.

These migrants, however, were primarily interested in Nebraska as a transit route, not as a destination in its own right. Although the United States had acquired Nebraska from France in 1803 through the Louisiana Purchase, settlement was slow to get off the ground. By the time of the California Gold Rush, the area was still largely unsettled.

Earlier in the century, the Missouri Fur Company had begun setting up trading posts along the Platte and Missouri rivers to trade with the Indians. In 1812, Spanish fur trapper

Did You Know?

Kool-Aid was invented in Nebraska in 1927. It is the official soft drink of the Cornhusker State.

and explorer Manuel Lisa built a trading post at Fort Lisa, near present-day Omaha. In 1822, the Missouri Fur Company established a permanent settlement in nearby Bellevue. This was the first town in Nebraska.

In the 1830s, however, Nebraska—like Kansas—had become a place to relocate Native Americans who lived in the lands east of the Mississippi River that the U.S. considered to be more desirable. To compensate, the federal government made it illegal for whites to settle in the areas west of the Mississippi—including Nebraska—that were now reserved for Indians.

The 1854 Kansas-Nebraska Act changed that. The organization of Nebraska into a territory officially opened it up for white settlement. Omaha, just north of the mouth of the Platte River, became the new territory's capital.

Territorial Nebraska originally included parts of present-day Colorado, North Dakota, South Dakota, Wyoming, and Montana. As these lands, in turn, became U.S. territories, Nebraska gradually shrank to its current size.

The impetus for making Nebraska a territory came from the push to create a *transcontinental* railroad. Westward expansion was continuing at a rapid rate. Establishing a rail connection along the Platte valley route would make the journey out west easier and faster. And with more and more people and goods passing through its borders, Nebraska was starting to become a destination in its own right.

 Did You Know?

Celebrated worldwide as a day to plant trees, Arbor Day was established in Nebraska in 1872. Today, in the United States, the holiday is observed on the final Friday in April.

In early 1854, U.S. Senator Stephen Douglas of Illinois introduced a bill in Congress that divided the land west of Missouri into two territories, Kansas and Nebraska. Both of these territories should have been "free" states under the terms of the 1820 Missouri Compromise, which had outlawed slavery above the 36° 30' latitude. However, Douglas proposed that settlers in each of the territories should decide whether slavery would be permitted, a doctrine he called "popular sovereignty." The legislation, officially titled "An Act to Organize the Territories of Nebraska and Kansas," reignited the national debate over slavery in the western territories.

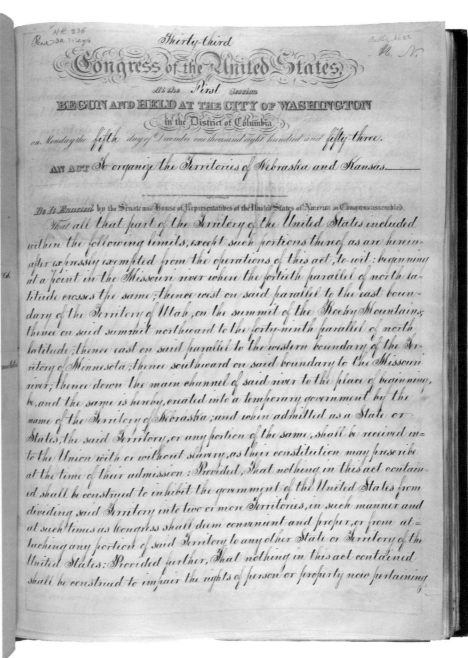

Directors of the Union Pacific Railroad pose with a train in central Nebraska, approximately 250 miles (402 km) west of Omaha, 1866. The spread of railroads helped open Nebraska to settlement in the late 19th century.

The Homestead Act of 1862 played a major role in these developments. This legislation allowed settlers to claim 160 acres of land from the federal government, practically for free. Thousands of settlers moved to Nebraska to cash in on the deal.

Nebraska's first homesteaders settled in the eastern and central parts of the territory, where the land and climate were more favorable for farming. Cattle ranchers settled in the west, where the grasslands of the prairie were perfect for grazing.

Early settlers faced many hardships, including shortages of water, fuel, and timber. At the time, only about three percent of Nebraska's terrain was forested. Without sufficient wood for building, many farmers had to construct homes from sod—clumps of matted soil and grass. These clumps of sod were nicknamed "prairie brick" or "Nebraska marble" by the early settlers. For fuel, they burned corncobs and dried buffalo dung.

Despite these hardships, Nebraska continued to grow at a fast rate. In 1854, just over 2,700 people lived in the newly formed territory. Most of these people lived in the east, in small clusters along the Missouri River. By 1867, however, Nebraska's population had spiked to 50,000. Omaha, Bellevue, Nebraska City, and other eastern river towns had become bustling cities. Settlers were also moving steadily deeper into the rest of the state.

Technological advances made this rapid growth possible. From wagon to

Cattle graze on the plains in northwestern Nebraska. During the 19th century, ranchers discovered that prairie grass was excellent for feeding livestock.

stagecoach and steamboat to railroad, innovations in transportation were opening up more and more of the frontier. By 1867, the whole of Nebraska was connected by railroad. By 1869, the transcontinental railroad was complete. Now, the entire country was connected by rail, coast to coast.

The railroads made it easier for settlers to populate more remote areas of Nebraska, including the western lands where cattle thrived. Railroads also gave the settlers access to a nation-wide market for their products. Nebraska's cattle industry boomed.

No battles were fought in Nebraska during the Civil War, but the territory indirectly contributed to the war effort by supplying beef to the Union Army. The war, in turn, boosted

Because wood and stone were hard to find on the prairie, many homesteaders in Nebraska built sod houses, using blocks of soil held together with thick-rooted prairie grass. This photo of a farm family in front of their sod house was taken around 1886.

Nebraska's cattle industry by creating an increased demand for the meat. By the late 1860s, Nebraska was America's top producer of beef.

Two years after the Civil War ended, Nebraska finally achieved statehood. Lancaster, renamed Lincoln after recently assassinated President Lincoln, became its new capital.

The state's proposed constitution originally included a clause restricting the right to vote to whites. As a result, Congress initially rejected Nebraska's bid for statehood. The Nebraska Legislature removed this restriction, and the territory entered the Union as the 37th state on March 1, 1867. Its state motto—"Equality before the law"—reflects this episode.

Although the Civil War had drawn to a close, a different conflict was intensifying in Nebraska—a conflict between the new settlers and the original inhabitants of the land.

Historically, the area that is now Nebraska was home to a number of different *indigenous* tribes, including the Pawnee, Omaha, Oto, Ponca, Lakota (Sioux), Cheyenne, and Arapaho.

The Pawnee were the largest Native American tribe in the area. At the time of the Louisiana Purchase, they numbered close to 10,000. They lived in central Nebraska, as did the Ponca. The Omaha and Oto lived primarily along the Missouri River, in eastern Nebraska. These tribes were *semi-sedentary*. For part of the year, they hunted buffalo. But for most of the year, they lived in permanent dwellings and raised crops.

The first person to file a claim for land under the Homestead Act of 1862 was Daniel Freeman, who claimed 160 acres in Nebraska. Today, the National Park Service maintains Homestead National Monument at the location of Freeman's claim. This national park includes a visitors center, where students can learn about homesteading and nature.

The Lakota, Cheyenne, and Arapaho were ***nomadic*** tribes living primarily in western Nebraska. Year-round, they migrated across the Plains, following herds of buffalo. They subsisted entirely off of hunting.

For the Native Americans, increased European-American settlement meant more competition for land and resources. The construction of the railroads and the development of the cattle industry meant the wholescale destruction of vast herds of buffalo. And as the buffalo disappeared from the Plains, the entire way of life of these tribes was threatened.

These tensions led to the outbreak of armed conflict between the U.S. Army and Nebraska's Lakota, Cheyenne, and Arapaho tribes. The clashes were part of a larger series of conflicts that took place throughout the Great Plains between about 1854 and 1890. They were a response to the ***encroachment*** onto Native American lands by European-American settlers. Collectively, these conflicts are known as the Plains Indian Wars.

This stone marker designates the spot where the famed Sioux chief Crazy Horse was killed at Fort Robinson, in northwestern Nebraska, in 1879.

Nebraska's last major campaign in the Plains Indian Wars was the Battle of Summit Springs in 1869, which was fought just outside Nebraska's border, in Colorado. However, minor skirmishes continued in Nebraska's panhandle until Lakota war chief Crazy Horse was killed in 1877 in the Pine Ridge region of northwestern Nebraska. By 1890, almost all of Nebraska's Native American tribes had ceded their lands to the U.S. government. They were moved to *reservations* in Oklahoma.

Government

In 1937, Nebraska became the only U.S. state with a unicameral, or single-house, legislature. The 49 members of this single assembly are called senators. They are elected to four-year terns, but are allowed by law to serve two consecutive terms.

Nebraska's state legislature is also unique in being the only *nonpartisan* state legislature in the nation. This means that candidates for election do not have their political party listed on the ballot.

Members of Nebraska's executive branch of government include the gov-

In February 2013, Nebraskans were surprised when longtime Lieutenant Governor Rick Sheehy (red shirt) resigned suddenly. It turned out that Sheehy had been involved in a scandal involving thousands of calls to four women using his state-issued cellphone.

The state capitol building in Lincoln houses the most important executive, judicial, and legislative offices of Nebraska's state government. The tower rises more than 400 feet (120 m), making it the tallest structure in Lincoln.

ernor, lieutenant governor, secretary of state, treasurer, and auditor. Each of these officials is elected to a four-year term.

Nebraska's Supreme Court is the highest court in the state's judicial branch. It consists of one chief justice and six associate justices. The governor initially appoints each justice. After the initial appointment period, justices must win the approval of voters to retain their seats.

President Barack Obama and U.S. Secretary of Defense Chuck Hagel place their hands over their hearts as the National Anthem is performed. Hagel was decorated for his military service during the Vietnam War, and later became a successful businessman. In 1997 he was elected to represent Nebraska in the U.S. Senate, a post he held until his retirement in 2009. In 2013, President Obama appointed Hagel to serve in his cabinet as Secretary of Defense.

Thanks to its relatively small population, Nebraska sends only three representatives to the U.S. House of Representatives. In presidential elections, Nebraska gets five electoral votes. Along with Maine, Nebraska is one of only two states that split their electoral votes by congressional district.

Because of this system, Democratic candidate Barack Obama ended up with one of Nebraska's electoral votes in the 2008 presidential election, even though Republican nominee John McCain carried the state as a whole. This was the first time since 1964 that this traditionally Republican state gave an electoral vote to a Democratic presidential nominee.

The Economy

Farming has been central to Nebraska's economy ever since its early days of statehood. Today, the Cornhusker State has about 45.5 million acres of farms and ranches. That's about 93 percent of the state's total land area. Overall, Nebraska ranks fourth in the nation for crop production, behind

California, Texas, and Iowa.

The first crop planted by Nebraska's settlers was corn. This is still the most widely grown crop in the state. According to the Nebraska Department of Agriculture, more than 8 million acres of land were planted with corn in 2012, yielding more than 1.2 billion bushels of the crop. Only Iowa and Illinois produce more corn than Nebraska.

Over 40 percent of the corn harvested in Nebraska goes to producing ethanol, an alcohol that can be blend-

The Union Pacific Railroad's Bailey Yard in North Platte is the world's busiest train yard. On average, 139 trains and over 14,000 railroad cars pass through Bailey Yard every day.

Farming is a major part of Nebraska's economy, and corn remains the state's primary crop.

ed with gasoline and used as fuel. Nebraska is the nation's second-largest producer of ethanol. It is America's top producer of beef, Great Northern beans, and popcorn.

Cattle, corn, soybeans, hogs, and wheat are Nebraska's top five *commodities*, in order of importance to the economy. Agriculture in general contributes over $21 billion every year to Nebraska's economy. That represents more than one-fifth of the state's total GDP, which exceeded $110 billion in 2014.

Manufacturing is another major revenue source for Nebraska. Farm equipment, fertilizers, pesticides, and medical instruments are among the top products manufactured in the state. Nebraska also leads in food manufacturing, with ConAgra, one of America's biggest packaged food companies, based here.

Nebraska's third-largest source of revenue is tourism, bringing in more than four billion dollars a year. Other important industries in the state include freight transport, telecommunications, and banking. A number of major insurance and financial institutions are based in Nebraska, including Mutual of Omaha and TD

Some Famous Nebraskans

Novelist Willa Cather (1873–1957) was born in Virginia but moved to Nebraska when she was ten. Best known for her novels O *Pioneers!* and *My Ántonia*, Cather chronicled frontier life in the Great Plains in several of her works.

Omaha-born dancer, musician, and actor Fred Astaire (1899–1987) was one of the greatest American stars of all time. He made his dancing debut with his older sister Adele Astaire (1896–1981) at age five, going on to perform in more than 30 musicals over the course of a career that spanned more than three-quarters of a century.

A number of A-list Hollywood actors have come from the Cornhusker State, including Henry Fonda (1905–1982), Marlon Brando (1924–2004), Nick Nolte (b. 1941), and Hilary Swank (b. 1974).

Church of Scientology founder L. Ron Hubbard (1911–1986) was born in Tilden, the same eastern Nebraska town that produced Phillies center fielder and Baseball Hall of Famer Richie Ashburn (1927–1997). Other ballplayers from Nebraska include Hall of Famers Wade Boggs (b. 1958) and Bob Gibson (b. 1935).

William Jennings Bryan (1860–1925) was a powerful figure in late 19th century and early 20th century politics, serving as U.S. Secretary of State and in the U.S. Congress. He was the Democratic Party's nominee for President in 1896, 1900, and 1908.

William Jennings Bryan

Other important political figures from Nebraska include 38th President of the United States Gerald Ford (1913–2006), African American civil rights activist Malcolm X (1925–1965), and Richard Cheney (b. 1941), vice president from 2001–2009 under George W. Bush.

Gerald Ford

Businessman Warren Buffett (b. 1930), nicknamed the "Oracle of Omaha" for his stock market insights, is one of the wealthiest men in the world, with a net worth valued at more than $67 billion in 2014.

Ameritrade. The Union Pacific Corporation, operator of the largest rail network in the United States, is also headquartered here.

The People

Nebraska is even less densely populated than Kansas. On average, there are fewer than 24 people per square mile in the state. The U.S. Census Bureau estimated 1,881,503 Cornhuskers in 2014, putting the state in 37th place for population. Over 50 percent of this population is clustered in just three eastern counties: Douglas, Lancaster, and Sarpy counties. Roughly one out of every three Nebraskans lives in Omaha and Lincoln, the state's two biggest cities.

Omaha is Nebraska's most diverse city. African Americans make up 13.7 percent of the city's population. That's slightly higher than the national average and almost three times greater than Nebraska's overall percentage. The city also has a sizable Mexican presence, and it is home to the nation's largest population of Sudanese refugees.

The rest of the state is significantly less diverse than both Omaha and the nation as a whole. According to the

Reconnaissance aircraft are parked on the flightline at Offutt Air Force Base near Omaha, Nebraska. The base, named for a World War I-era pilot from Nebraska, is home to the U.S. Strategic Command, which is responsible for using nuclear weapons in war when ordered by the president.

Fans cheer at a University of Nebraska football game at Memorial Stadium in Lincoln. The 87,000-seat stadium has sold out more than 340 consecutive games. The Nebraska Cornhuskers are one of college football's most storied football programs and have won five national championships.

2010 Census, white Nebraskans make up 89.7 percent of the state's total population. That's 12 percent higher than the national average. Just 2 percent of Nebraskans are Asian, compared to 5.3 percent for the U.S. as a whole.

Nebraskans of Hispanic or Latino heritage make up 9.2 percent of the state's population—almost half the national average. However, Hispanics are the fastest growing ethnic group in the state. Over the next three and a half decades, their numbers are expected to more than triple, reaching a projected 24 percent of the total population by 2050.

Currently, German Americans make up Nebraska's largest ethnic group, followed by Irish and English.

Nebraska has the largest proportion of Czech Americans in the nation. Many of them live in the southeastern town of Wilber, nicknamed the "Czech Capital of the U.S.A."

Major Cities

With a population of about 410,000, *Omaha* is Nebraska's biggest city. Until the 1990s, the city was home to the Union Stockyards, once the largest livestock market and meat-packing industry in the nation. Today, Omaha is a major business hub, boasting several companies on Fortune magazine's list of America's top 500 corporations. Included on that list is Berkshire Hathaway, the multinational investment firm run by billionaire Warren Buffett, an Omaha native.

Roughly 55 miles southwest of Omaha is *Lincoln*, Nebraska's capital

Aerial view of Omaha, the state's largest city.

View of downtown Lincoln, including St. Mary Catholic Church, founded in 1867.

The ranch and home owned by famed Western showman Buffalo Bill Cody is now a state park near North Platte.

and second largest city. About a quarter of a million Nebraskans live here. According to a 2013 Gallup-Healthways survey, Lincoln residents are the healthiest and happiest in the nation.

Fur traders in the early 19th century appreciated *Bellevue's* pleasant scenery and gave the city its name—meaning "beautiful view" in French. Today, Bellevue is Nebraska's oldest and third-largest city (population 50,200). During World War II, factories in Bellevue assembled B-29 bombers for the U.S. military, including the ones that that dropped atomic bombs on Japan in August 1945.

Almost 25,000 people live in *North Platte*, according to the U.S. Census Bureau. But although the southwestern Nebraska city is only the eighth-largest in the state, it is the site of the largest train yard in the world. The 2,850-acre facility at Bailey Yard manages up to 14,000 rail cars a day. Back in the 1880s, North Platte was home to Buffalo Bill Cody—famed Pony Express rider, buffalo hunter, U.S. Army scout, and

Gavins Point Dam is a hydroelectric dam on the Missouri River near the border with South Dakota. It created Lewis and Clark Lake, a popular vacation spot for tourists.

Wild West showman. Today, his former residence is a historical park and museum filled with memorabilia from his life and times.

Eighty-nine percent of Nebraska's cities have fewer than 3,000 residents. Hundreds of towns have populations smaller than 1,000. But even in a state with so many small cities and towns, tiny **Monowi** in central Nebraska is remarkable. As of the 2010 U.S. Census, the town's population is 1. This makes Monowi the smallest incorporated town in the nation.

Further Reading

Heinrichs, Ann. *Nebraska*. New York: Children's Press, 2014.

Owen, David. *Like No Other Place: The Sandhills of Nebraska*. Lincoln: University of Nebraska Press, 2012.

Partsch, Tammy. *It Happened in Nebraska: Remarkable Events That Shaped History*. Guilford, Conn.: Globe Pequot Press, 2012

Internet Resources

http://nebraskahistory.org/index.shtml

The home page of the Nebraska Historical Society has information about Nebraska's history, as well as online exhibits on many topics related to the state.

http://www.visitnebraska.com/

The Nebraska Tourism Commission provides this online guide to sights and cities in the Cornhusker State.

http://www.nebraskastudies.org

Browse photos, videos, maps, timelines, and more to learn about Nebraska's history from the 16th century to the present.

http://www.nebraskaflyway.com/index.php

Learn about the sandhill cranes that flock to Nebraska's Platte River, one of the most spectacular congregations of migrating birds anywhere on the planet.

 # Text-Dependent Questions

1. What is the Ogallala Aquifer? How is it important to Nebraska?
2. What role did railroads play in Nebraska's settlement and development?
3. What is unique about Nebraska's state legislature?

 # Research Project

Nebraska's early settlers had to cope with many challenges, including droughts, grasshopper infestations, and dust storms. Using the Internet or your school library, learn more about what life was like for Nebraska's pioneers. Try to find first-hand accounts of 19th-century life on the prairie.

Index

Numbers in **bold italics** refer to captions.

Series Glossary of Key Terms

bicameral—having two legislative chambers (for example, a senate and a house of representatives).

cede—to yield or give up land, usually through a treaty or other formal agreement.

census—an official population count.

constitution—a written document that embodies the rules of a government.

delegation—a group of persons chosen to represent others.

elevation—height above sea level.

legislature—a lawmaking body.

precipitation—rain and snow.

term limit—a legal restriction on how many consecutive terms an office holder may serve.